THE SWORD
OF THE
SPIRIT IN MEMORY

Easy Method to Memorize Scripture

Combination devotional, journal, and arranged scriptures for
memorization of basic *foundational* scriptures that every believer
should have memorized for a solid, victorious Christian life.

TENA MARCHAND

WESTBOW
PRESS
A DIVISION OF THOMAS NELSON

Scripture quotations taken from the New American Standard Bible, unless otherwise noted.
Copyright © 1960, 1962, 1963, 1968, 1971, 1972, 1973,
1975, 1977, 1995 by The Lockman Foundation
Used by permission. (www.Lockman.org)

WestBow Press books may be ordered through booksellers or by contacting:

WestBow Press
A Division of Thomas Nelson
1663 Liberty Drive
Bloomington, IN 47403
www.westbowpress.com
1-(866) 928-1240

Because of the dynamic nature of the Internet, any web addresses or links contained in this book may have changed since publication and may no longer be valid. The views expressed in this work are solely those of the author and do not necessarily reflect the views of the publisher, and the publisher hereby disclaims any responsibility for them.

Any people depicted in stock imagery provided by Thinkstock are models, and such images are being used for illustrative purposes only.

Certain stock imagery © Thinkstock.

ISBN: 978-1-4497-4138-9 (sc)
ISBN: 978-1-4497-4139-6 (e)

Library of Congress Control Number: 2012903546

Printed in the United States of America

WestBow Press rev. date: 10/11/2012

DEDICATION

On behalf of God Himself, this book is dedicated to all believers, without exception—from the new believer who wants to start right and stay right, to the long-time Christian who wants to be set free from years of defeat in his or her walk with the Lord. It's also dedicated to the Christian who never developed a routine for memorizing scripture on a continual basis.

The Lord gave me a method to memorize His Word, and I really believe He meant for me to pass it along to the Body of Christ. These are well-rounded *foundational* scriptures, very basic and necessary, for your transformation into God's image and for maintaining a strong commitment to Him. As you forsake your ways and adopt His with this assortment of scriptures, you will keep your heart pure and live in peace, joy, and freedom.

PREFACE

Scripture memorization has been one of my biggest weaknesses as a Christian. It has been a difficult *chore*. The easiest times for memorizing scripture were during trials, as the Word ministered to my needs. Or I have read certain scriptures many times over the years; and they read in such a way that they were automatically memorized without any conscious effort or plan to do so.

As I was on my daily walk, a detailed plan for simplifying this process entered my mind out of nowhere—I was not thinking about this subject at all. Without any doubt, I knew that it was God-given. To have a successful Christian life, memorization of His Word is *vital*. Not only is it our transformation into His likeness, but it is the sword of the Spirit put into action against *all* attacks of the enemy (Ephesians 6:17). The earlier we start to memorize and meditate on scripture, the quicker and easier we will be set free from habits and bondage. Many of us have been Christians for years, but have not developed a permanent routine for memorizing a variety of passages that address the issues of life. Without this, we limit all that God intends for us to have, and do, and be.

The Word is also your shield of faith. You are building two very important parts of the armor of God—the sword and the shield. His Word is our offense and defense against satan (I'd rather not capitalize his name). As I studied the shield of faith, I discovered some real eye-openers. Briefly, a few comments are worth sharing as encouragement to strengthen your commitment to memorizing scripture:

From the description of the physical shield in Fausset's Bible Dictionary, I was able to see the parallel to our spiritual shield of faith:

- The shield involved two soldiers. One handled the shield, rocking it back and forth, protecting the other soldier. This freed him to go on the offensive or defensive without his having to maneuver the heavy, whole-body shield.
- The shield was made red to strike terror into the foe: we are covered by the Blood of Jesus, which strikes terror into satan.
- The surface was kept bright with oil, preserving the leather and the metal: oil references the Holy Spirit and the anointing. Not only does His brightness blind satan, but we also have the anointing of the Holy Spirit.
- The shield was covered when not in use: we have the Word hidden in our hearts, ready for use. As stated in Psalms 119:11, "Thy Word I have treasured in my heart..."

- "Out with the shield!" was their shout in response to war: when satan attacks, we are "out with the Word," drawing from the appropriate scripture(s) we have memorized and stored in our hearts. It is our weapon—the sword, the Word of God—with which to put the enemy to flight.
- The shield was carried by another soldier who would go before the warrior: our faith goes before us for victory over satan.

We read in 1 Chronicles 12:8, "And from the Gadites there came over to David in the stronghold in the wilderness, mighty men of valor, men trained for war, who could handle shield and spear, and whose faces were like the faces of lions, and they were as swift as the gazelles on the mountains." As you can see, these warriors were impressively strong, courageous, and skilled; they were very fast, well-trained, and completely able—a real terror in battle. Strategically, the enemy aimed at their shield for destruction. If this were accomplished, it would render them access to these great men who, once the shield was removed, would be very limited with inadequate protection. In this reference, one of the Hebrew meanings for "shield" is "target." I realized our faith—"shield of faith"—is the target of satan! He relentlessly throws those fiery darts (Ephesians 6:16) at our shield of faith in an attempt to weaken us until we surrender and become defeated. He wants to destroy our faith. Don't lose heart. Be encouraged by the following paragraph.

Our faith is a must. Jesus tells us to have faith in God. When you think you are doubting, you may NOT be. In Mark 11:23, Jesus said he that "does not doubt in his heart, but believes..." We do believe in our hearts; but satan tries to inflict doubt and temptations into our minds, where we feel the battle. The force against our faith can be so strong that we perceive it as doubt. Imagine holding a big shield in front of you. It's big enough to cover all the other parts of your armor, keeping them hidden and protected from the enemy. He will throw massive objects at your shield in order to knock it down—exposing the rest of the armor, and ultimately you, to destruction. Although it's an impressive attack, your shield (faith) is not destroyed or damaged. The other parts of the armor are not even touched—and neither are you. When satan suggests thoughts of doubt, we feel it; but they're only suggestions. Don't fall for the lie that you're doubting. Keep your shield up. Take your sword of the Spirit from your arsenal of memorized verses hidden in your heart. Use it to resist satan. Understand that you must get your scriptures and quote them every time you have a doubt sensation—you will have built your faith to the extent that doubt is no longer a problem in your particular area of need. satan's effect is diminished; he is rendered null, void, and powerless. When he attempts to attack you in that area again, cut him off immediately. Perhaps he needs just a mere reminder this time.

satan will even withdraw his temptations when you continue to stand on your scripture(s). We are instructed in James 4:7, "Submit therefore to God. Resist the devil and he will flee from you." When Jesus was at the end of His forty days of fasting in the desert, probably His weakest time, satan thought he had the perfect opportunity to destroy His steadfast obedience to God. Jesus was presented with temptations in three very enticing areas, but He countered with the appropriate scripture for each one (Luke 4:1–13). He first submitted to God, rather than the temptation, by obeying the Word. This then empowered Him to resist satan, leaving him no choice but to flee, a complete failure. As you strive to submit to God and resist satan, you can have this very same result when tempted—even in your most vulnerable moment.

INTRODUCTION

With this method of memorizing scripture, you will concentrate on only a short portion of scripture each day. Write only the phrase being memorized on a sticky note or an index card and carry it with you. It will not be difficult to remember just a few words at a time in its written order—you may not even need to write it down. This short phrase will have a single, concentrated thought. You will be focusing on the meaning of each word and, of course, the phrase itself. Take it apart word-by-word and focus on each word individually. You will be surprised at the impact this has. Alternate your emphasis on different words and word-groupings throughout the day. Quote the whole phrase, then focus on the meaning of a single word; quote the whole phrase again, focusing on a different word's meaning. Repeat this cycle as you are able. The clearer the passage becomes, the easier it is to memorize. And more importantly, the truth of it begins to take root in your life. Your mind is being renewed. Once you know it, continue to quote it. At the end of the day, read the whole verse—just read, not working on memory. I've heard it said that the last five words you think about in your day are the most important. Every night, just before drifting off to sleep, quote all of your current verse that you have memorized thus far.

NOTE: If you experience a busy season, and you are unable to memorize your phrase for the day, don't get discouraged. Pick it up the next day—just don't give up! If you persist, it will become a habit like anything else that's a routine part of your life. You can work on your scripture during a few of your daily activities, such as brushing your teeth, showering, washing dishes, doing yard work, putting up groceries, walking (my favorite), running, biking, getting water to drink (eight to ten glasses a day), waiting for your PC to reboot, or anytime you have a few minutes of walking to get from one place to another, etc. You may come up with numerous other activities that will suffice. Perhaps there is someone with whom you are very close, and you can invite them as a buddy in your endeavor. Tape your verse on your bathroom mirror so that you will see it first thing in the morning and when retiring in the evening.

For those of you with smart phones, I downloaded the Bible on mine. It's so easy to pull up a scripture verse in my favorite Bible version and take a picture of it within the phone. I can select it from my camera roll at anytime until it's memorized. This works really well for me. And when the lights are out, I can verify accuracy of my scripture on my phone before I fall asleep. I also use it to record longer segments of scripture and listen to it when I awaken, before getting out of bed.

I believe the phrases are arranged for easy memorization. If you find that any are a little long, shorten it as works for you (I don't think this will happen very often).

Here's an example of a scripture verse set up for memory, with a few accompanying thoughts for meditation:

Day 1: "For God so loved the world" (Note: quotations for scriptures to be memorized are used in the example scripture only.)

"For God"—God, the Almighty, not any human being.
"so"—It emphasizes the *demonstration* and extent of His love for us.
"loved"—This is not just a feeling, but an action that He carried out. Love acts; it's not just words.
"so loved"—He *demonstrated* His love in a certain manner and to a certain depth.
"the world"—This includes every single person ever to be created. No one, by any degree of sin, is excluded from His love.
"For God so loved the world"

On Day 2, learn the second phrase. It's divided into several segments of one or more words that flow together well. Shuffle the segments around for meditation and memorization throughout the day. Periodically quote the entire phrase. Repeat this cycle until you know it.

Day 2: "that He gave His only begotten Son"

"that He gave"—God voluntarily gave His only Son to be crucified for our sins. Otherwise, we would all be hell-bound. God fulfilled His part in making Heaven possible to us; we have an absolute responsibility to fulfill our part. Our own goodness won't suffice.
"His only"—Jesus was all that He had.
"that He gave His only"
"begotten"—Jesus became a human being for a purpose. He was subject to human weakness just as we are, but never sinned when tempted. Yet, He took the punishment for *our* guilt of sin.
"that He gave His only begotten"
"His only begotten Son"
"Son"—Your children are a part of you and when anything happens to them, a part of you is ripped out. What sorrow and grief God must have had. (Could you offer your loved one to die a brutal death for the worst of sinners, if it were their only way to Heaven?)
"that He gave His only begotten Son"

Every other day or so, connect all of the phrases you have learned thus far. You will begin to see the strength of the verse, and its application to your life will be sharper and more powerful. It's not just words that you are memorizing. It's His Word, alive and active—very effective in your life.

On Day 3, combine Days 1 and 2. They are both memorized; meditate on it during the day. And continue to quote it.

Day 3: "For God so loved the world, that He gave His only begotten Son"

(*On the following page I became wordy; but I'm not suggesting such deep thought, unless that's your tendency. Otherwise, keep it simple and adequate.)

Day 4: "that whoever believes in Him"

"that"—A purpose. The act of giving His only Son meets a particular need.
"whoever"—It's open to all; He makes no distinction. He doesn't love one more than the other. (Think about how He loves your offenders, or those with whom you have serious issues. Unite your heart with His for them.)
"believes in Him"—This is not merely believing in His *existence*. It means obedience to His written plan of salvation with a real desire to stop sinning. People follow what they believe, and it affects their lives. True belief in Him always produces Godly changes.
"that whoever believes in Him"

Day 5:   "For God so loved the world, that He gave His only begotten Son, that whoever believes in Him"

Day 6: "should not perish, but have eternal life."

"should"—Something ordinarily expected or destined to occur.
"not"—Prevented from happening or being.
"perish"—Destroyed, lost. Eternally in hell.
"should not perish"
"but have"—God offers you the alternative to a destiny of perishing. To have it, you must receive it; and it must be received on His terms.
"should not perish, but have"
"eternal"—Forever, never ending. In Heaven you cannot compromise your commitment to Jesus. You are safely His forever! satan is bound in hell and has no access to you. Hell is eternal, too; once there, no one can ever come out. (We think we're okay as we are. I had this misconception—if people would just read the Bible, with an open and seeking heart, to see what it takes to get to Heaven!)
"life"—Not life as we know it. There are no temptations, jealousies, hardships, deaths, trials, sicknesses, strife, tiredness, etc. There are no discomforts of any sort. We will enjoy pure Godly ecstasy, as we are surrounded by His glory, holiness, magnificence, etc. We will be filled with joy, peace, happiness, and all of God's very nature. Best of all, we will be with Jesus and have fellowship with Him forever and ever.
"but have eternal life"
"should not perish, but have eternal life"

Day 7:   John 3:16 "For God so loved the world, that He gave His only begotten Son, that whoever believes in Him should not perish, but have eternal life."

Never allow your heart to become cold to this—ever! The work done on the Cross is effective for a *repentant* heart only. That's not a one-time act, but a way of life until you enter Heaven. Many think that intellectual belief in Jesus is salvation. James 2:19 says, "You believe that God is one. You do well; the demons also believe, and shudder." They know that He exists and they know very well Who He is; but they will NOT be in Heaven. Salvation "belief" is giving your life to Him and forsaking the *practice* of sin. (Be sure you are reading your Bible, not only to build a relationship with God, but also to learn what the Bible calls sin, so that you can turn away from it.) As you read the Word and follow His ways, you are allowing Jesus to actually live through you.

There's only one of two ways to pay for your sins: (1) Acknowledge that you are born sin-stained like everybody else and that you need redemption. Repent of the sins—this is to confess *and turn away from sin*. If you fall again, God is merciful and will pick you up *as many times as it takes* until you are free. He understands weakness (Romans 6-8). But He also recognizes pure, willful disobedience. Take Song of Solomon 2:15 to heart as well; "...(it's the) little foxes that are ruining the vineyards." The tiniest of sin, *harbored*, is as damaging as "big" obvious sins. Sin is sin. Don't let anything put or keep a barrier between you and God. Love and obey Him with all of your heart. (2) The other way is to pay for it yourself by spending *eternity* in hell.

Please—memorize this one first, and forever embrace it! *Know* the sacrifice. If there were just one sinner on earth, Jesus would have gone through all the brutal torture and crucifixion in His desperate love for that one person, even if they were to reject it. He did it because it's our *only* way to Heaven. No one can call God unloving for anyone's being in hell—He doesn't want anyone to go there. He paid a high price to spare us from such a horrific consequence. It's a free gift to us. The choice to take it or leave it is ours. We alone, *through our own wills,* choose our destiny.

After each scripture is a blank page to record *your* insights, prayers, and testimonies of how the Lord used the scripture in your life as a result of memorizing it. Jot down your thoughts and how the scriptures minister to you. (Unless otherwise noted, all verses are in New American Standard. Ample space is provided for you to write the scriptures in your favorite Bible version.)

Some of the passages may take two or more weeks to memorize due to its length, or the wording being a little tricky to put together. They happen to be key verses deserving of a little extra time, to really get it embedded in your spirit. Occasionally, we just have to park at a certain place with the Lord, in order to cultivate deep roots for that particular scripture. When satan comes like a roaring lion, seeking to devour you with assignments against you, you will stand firm as you draw from the appropriate memorized verse in the hidden places of your heart. It's your sword of the Spirit with which to fight and defeat him.

You are prepared for effective memorization of scripture for victory in Christ. I pray this journey be strong and consistent.

So, One-so-loved-of-God, lets get started!

NOTE: Acts 15:8, the Holy Spirit is a gift that God gives to us. Familiarize yourself with some of His functions in these verses. 2 Corinthians 13:14, we have fellowship with Him. Jude 20, we can pray in the Holy Spirit. Acts 1:8, He empowers us. Mark 13:11, He will speak through us in critical moments when we fear what to say. Luke 12:12, He will also teach you what to say. Acts 16:6, He forbids us to speak at times. Luke 2:26, He will give us revelations. John 14:26, He will teach us all things and bring to remembrance what He taught. Acts 13:4, He directs us. Hebrews 10:15, He also bears witness to us. Acts 20:28, He makes you what you are. Romans 5:5, He pours out God's love within our hearts. Ephesians 4:30, He can be grieved. In 1 Thessalonians 5:19, we are told not to quench the Holy Spirit. He's a gift, but we must voluntarily give Him His place.

2 Corinthians 5:17 Therefore if any man is in Christ, he is a new creature; the old things passed away; behold, new things have come.

As Christians, we are always in a battle between the old nature and the new nature. Our old nature is the one with which we were born. It sins very easily and naturally. When we take Jesus into our lives as Savior, we receive the new nature, which is Jesus Himself in us. He cannot sin. When temptations come, our own wills go either way—new nature renewal or old nature tendencies (sin). For years, when October or November would come around, my Christian commitments would begin to dwindle. I would get discouraged and just couldn't wait for the new year, so I could start fresh again. Then one day this verse ministered to me. I am a new creature. Any time we confess our sins, we are just as if we had not sinned, flawless before God. We must always stay repentant, allowing the new nature to replace our old nature and its sinful habits. I also realized that before I was a Christian, I celebrated New Year's Resolutions. This tradition, along with the failure pattern, carried over into my Christian experience—starting out right, seeing the commitments dwindle in October, and waiting for the new year for a fresh start. Thankfully, I am renewed to a state of righteousness before God any time I confess my sins.

Day 1: Therefore if any man is in Christ,

Day 2: he is a new creature,

Day 3: Therefore if any man is in Christ, he is a new creature,

Day 4: the old things passed away,

Day 5: behold, new things have come.

Day 6: the old things passed away; behold, new things have come.

Day 7: 2 Corinthians 5:17 Therefore if any man is in Christ, he is a new creature; the old things passed away; behold, new things have come.

THOUGHTS, PRAYERS, AND TESTIMONIES

_____

_____

_____

_____

_____

_____

_____

_____

_____

_____

_____

_____

_____

_____

_____

_____

_____

_____

Romans 12:2 And do not be conformed to this world, but be transformed by the renewing of your mind, that you may prove what the will of God is, that which is good and acceptable and perfect.

In Christ, we *are* new and perfect creatures. But we must constantly be changed in thought, word, and deed to be a *manifested* new creature. We do not just become perfect in our ways overnight. As long as we are on this earth, we will have our old nature which is prone to sin. Temptations and weaknesses will always be pulling at us. Every habit we have today started with a thought—we are products of what we think. As new creatures, we must change our way of thinking. It may be easy to follow the ways of the world if we are not careful. Many of the changes we will be making will take more than "willpower", which is just a matter of our own struggle against sin that usually ends in defeat and discouragement. Rather, becoming more and more sinless is a matter of "renewing" our minds with scripture. And we do that by meditation on and memorization of His Word, with a heart to obey. Hence, we develop new patterns of ingrained thought resulting in new habits—the new creature revealed!

Day 1: And do not be conformed to this world,

Day 2: but be transformed

Day 3: And do not be conformed to this world, but be transformed

Day 4: by the renewing of your mind

Day 5: And do not be conformed to this world, but be transformed by the renewing of your mind

(verse continued)

Tena Marchand

THOUGHTS, PRAYERS, AND TESTIMONIES

Day 1: that you may prove

Day 2: what the will of God is,

Day 3: that you may prove what the will of God is

Day 4: And do not be conformed to this world, but be transformed by the renewing of your mind, that you may prove what the will of God is

Day 5: that which is good and acceptable and perfect.

Day 6: that you may prove what the will of God is, that which is good and acceptable and perfect.

Day 7: Romans 12:2 And do not be conformed to this world, but be transformed by the renewing of your mind, that you may prove what the will of God is, that which is good and acceptable and perfect.

Romans 12:1: I urge you therefore, brethren, by the mercies of God, to present your bodies a living and holy sacrifice, acceptable to God, which is your spiritual service of worship.

This is one of the verses I stand on for the healings and miracles I need in my body. For the things I've endured that need God's miraculous touch, I *literally* offer my body a living sacrifice for healing *for His glory* as an avenue to reveal Himself to a lost and dying world!

THOUGHTS, PRAYERS, AND TESTIMONIES

Jeremiah 31:3 The LORD appeared to him from afar, saying, "I have loved you with an everlasting love; therefore I have drawn you with loving-kindness".

We all came into this world sin-stained and cannot enter Heaven in this condition. God is so Holy. Any sin, however "small" in our eyes, puts an infinite distance between God and us. But no matter how far we are from Him, even if guilty of the worst of all sins, His love reaches out to us in some way to rescue us from eternal separation from Him. His love is everlasting and nothing can destroy or lessen it. Only we, of our own choice, can reject or walk away from that unconditional love. In spite of any sin, His loving-kindness endures toward us. Never let the enemy influence you with any other thought of God's love for you. It is desperate enough to give His only Son Jesus—totally innocent of any guilt or sin—to die in your place. He loves you just as much as anyone, no matter what. And remember, there is not a thing on this earth you can do to deserve His love. Sadly, some people think they have to turn from some of their sins *before* they can come to Him. He has no such requirement. Any turning away from sin without Him as Lord and Savior merits you nothing. Simply acknowledge you are born a sinner like every other person on this earth. Accept that Jesus took the punishment for your sins, sparing you from eternity in hell. And make Him Savior and Lord of your life. He wants you to come to Him just as you are. And beautifully, the changes will start with Him in your life. Even after you fail Him once you're a Christian, confess it and get back on track. He loves you! Get to the place where you are letting Him live in you.

Day 1: The Lord appeared to him from afar, saying,

Day 2: "I have loved you with an everlasting love,

Day 3: The LORD appeared to him from afar, saying, "I have loved you with an everlasting love;

Day 4: therefore I have drawn you

Day 5: The Lord appeared to him from afar, saying, "I have loved you with an everlasting love; therefore I have drawn you

Day 6: therefore I have drawn you with loving-kindness".

Day 7: Jeremiah 31:3 The Lord appeared to him from afar, saying, "I have loved you with an everlasting love; therefore I have drawn you with loving-kindness".

TENA MARCHAND

THOUGHTS, PRAYERS, AND TESTIMONIES

_____

_____

_____

_____

_____

_____

_____

_____

_____

_____

_____

_____

_____

_____

_____

_____

_____

Ps 86:12 I will give thanks to Thee, O Lord my God, with all my heart, and will glorify Thy name forever.

Develop these precious priorities with your Heavenly Father. Make it a priority to faithfully give Him thanks—not only for what He has already done, but you can thank Him beforehand as you pray for your needs. I can't stress enough the importance of making your heart a thankful heart. It will prevent many hard attitudes from taking root in your life. It allows Him to move on your behalf more easily. Make it a priority to glorify His name at all times, to praise Him daily. Give Him a devoted portion of your day, no matter how small, with Him as your only focus. Make it a priority to remember His loving-kindness. Periodically recall the things He has done for you, and never take His favor for granted. Guard from turning away from your first Love. We have to build on that relationship to keep it strong. It protects you from satan's subtle efforts to gradually minimize your relationship with God—with the intent of total destruction.

Day 1: I will give thanks to Thee.

Day 2: O Lord My God.

Day 3: I will give thanks to Thee, O Lord my God,

Day 4: with all my heart,

Day 5: and will glorify Thy name forever.

Day 6: with all my heart, and will glorify Thy name forever.

Day 7: I will give thanks to Thee, O Lord my God, with all my heart, and will glorify Thy name forever.

Take note of this verse as well: 1 Thessalonians 5:16–17 Rejoice always; (17) pray without ceasing; (18) in everything give thanks; for this is God's will for you in Christ Jesus.

THOUGHTS, PRAYERS, AND TESTIMONIES

_____

_____

_____

_____

_____

_____

_____

_____

_____

_____

_____

_____

_____

_____

_____

_____

_____

_____

James 1:2–3 Consider it all joy, my brethren, when you encounter various trials, (3) knowing that the testing of your faith produces endurance.

I remember in my early days as a Christian, waking up in the middle of the night, quoting several verses around this scripture—but I never committed them to memory. I assumed that I was getting ready to go through a hardship, and the Lord was preparing me. Since then, at the onset of trials, I have learned to say, "Lord, I consider it all joy (a 'calm delight' in Him), because I know You will work something of Yourself into me." We are primed in these times for Godly changes, an increase in our faith, and a stronger relationship with Him. During an extended period of a frightening situation in the past, the intimacy with God was so wonderful, that with all sincerity of heart, I afterward whispered, "Lord, I'd be willing to go through it all over again—just for what I had with You."

Day 1: Consider it all joy, my brethren,

Day 2: when you encounter various trials,

Day 3: Consider it all joy, my brethren, when you encounter various trials,

Day 4: (3) knowing that the testing of your faith

Day 5: produces endurance

Day 6: (3) knowing that the testing of your faith produces endurance.

Day 7: James 1:2–3 Consider it all joy, my brethren, when you encounter various trials, (3) knowing that the testing of your faith produces endurance.

THOUGHTS, PRAYERS, AND TESTIMONIES

Romans 8:28 And we know that God causes all things to work together for good to those who love God, to those who are called according to His purpose.

I love this promise. Life is filled with both good and bad experiences. We can all make a two-column list of every positive and negative that we've encountered. We will ultimately be able to extract something good from each negative and place it in the positive column. This is not to minimize the pain, suffering, and lingering effects of severe trials; but some of our most precious and priceless treasures are results from our most difficult times. Even though it may take a long time to manifest, you will eventually see His Word prove true—you will be able to recognize something good released to you from that trial. If we aren't able to see it on this earth, we will have a clear understanding of the "why," with gratitude, once we get to Heaven. When you're disappointed with the turn of events in your life, look to God and thank Him for what He has in store. Tell Him you trust Him.

Day 1: And we know that God causes all things

Day 2: to work together for good

Day 3: And we know that God causes all things to work together for good

Day 4: to those who love God,

Day 5: And we know that God causes all things to work together for good to those who love God,

Day 6: to those who are called

Day 7: And we know that God causes all things to work together for good to those who love God, to those who are called

(verse continued)

THOUGHTS, PRAYERS, AND TESTIMONIES

_____

_____

_____

_____

_____

_____

_____

_____

_____

_____

_____

_____

_____

_____

_____

_____

_____

_____

_____

Day 1: according to His purpose.

Day 2: to those who are called according to His purpose.

Day 3: Romans 8:28 And we know that God causes all things to work together for good to those who love God, to those who are called according to His purpose.

When you have these extra days without arranged scripture, you can go over those already memorized that may need a little refreshing. Perhaps as you meditate on this particular one, you may want to take a few days to make that two-column list of the things that God has turned around for your good.

THOUGHTS, PRAYERS, AND TESTIMONIES

_____

_____

_____

_____

_____

_____

_____

_____

_____

_____

_____

_____

_____

_____

_____

_____

_____

1 Corinthians 10:13 No temptation has overtaken you but such as is common to man; and God is faithful, Who will not allow you to be tempted beyond what you are able, but with the temptation will provide the way of escape also, that you may be able to endure it.

Before I was a Christian, I thought my life reflected a "good standard" of character. After I became a Christian, the more I read my Bible, the uglier my "little sins" became. I can remember saying, "Lord, there's no way anyone else has these kinds of temptations and sins." But you know what? Nothing new will ever be invented by you or me. Everybody has the same potential for all sins. The more we memorize *and apply* scripture, the less accessible our old nature is to the enemy of our souls. For every temptation and habit, there's scripture available for combat, resulting in solid life-change. Praying the Word engages God in your fight. Be aware that temptations can get so strong that it may *feel* like you've sinned—and when it bombards you, you *think* you have. Not so! You are resisting, and sometimes it takes a lot of effort to fight certain temptations. Be encouraged. You will see the fruit of your labors as you faithfully resist with the Word. satan will realize his defeat and flee *with* the temptation.

Day 1: No temptation has overtaken you

Day 2: but such as is common to man

Day 3: No temptation has overtaken you but such as is common to man

Day 4: And God is faithful,

Day 5: Who will not allow you to be tempted

Day 6: and God is faithful, Who will not allow you to be tempted

Day 7: No temptation has overtaken you but such as is common to man; and God is faithful, Who will not allow you to be tempted

(verse continued)

TENA MARCHAND

THOUGHTS, PRAYERS, AND TESTIMONIES

_____

_____

_____

_____

_____

_____

_____

_____

_____

_____

_____

_____

_____

_____

_____

_____

Day 1: beyond what you are able

Day 2: and God is faithful, Who will not allow you to be tempted beyond what you are able

Day 3: No temptation has overtaken you but such as is common to man; and God is faithful, Who will not allow you to be tempted beyond what you are able

Day 4: but with the temptation will provide the way of escape also,

Day 5: that you may be able to endure it.

Day 6: but with the temptation will provide the way of escape also that you may be able to endure it.

Day 7: 1 Corinthians 10:13 No temptation has overtaken you but such as is common to man; and God is faithful, who will not allow you to be tempted beyond what you are able, but with the temptation will provide the way of escape also, that you may be able to endure it.

THOUGHTS, PRAYERS, AND TESTIMONIES

_____

_____

_____

_____

_____

_____

_____

_____

_____

_____

_____

_____

_____

_____

_____

_____

_____

_____

James 4:7 Submit therefore to God. Resist the devil and he will flee from you.

It is imperative to realize that when temptation comes, it is not just your willpower that will do the job of resisting. Jesus was our example in Luke 4:1–13. For forty days, He was in the desert fasting. He ate and drank nothing. satan approached Jesus at His most vulnerable time of the fast. But in response to each compelling temptation presented, Jesus first submitted to God; then He quoted the Word to satan. After his third attempt, he fled. Jesus stood His ground in the Word—the very force and success behind His resistance. When you consistently turn from your own desire and submit to God's ways, you are allowing Him to actually live through you. At some point, He takes over to the degree that the temptation itself has no influence over you. satan cannot refuse Jesus. For every need encountered, keep adding to your arsenal of scripture. In all of our temptations, we are submitting to one and resisting the other. When we choose to sin, we are submitting to satan and resisting God. The next verse says, "Draw near to God and He will draw near to you." The nearer He comes to you and the more you allow Him to live through you, the easier it is to resist temptation.

Day 1: Submit therefore to God

Day 2: Resist the devil

Day 3: Submit therefore to God. Resist the devil

Day 4: and he will flee from you.

Day 5: Resist the devil and he will flee from you

Day 6: James 4:7 Submit therefore to God. Resist the devil and he will flee from you.

THOUGHTS, PRAYERS, AND TESTIMONIES

_____

_____

_____

_____

_____

_____

_____

_____

_____

_____

_____

_____

_____

_____

_____

_____

_____

Ephesians 6:12 For our struggle is not against flesh and blood, but against the rulers, against the powers, against the world forces of this darkness, against the spiritual forces of wickedness in the heavenly places.

To know this and act on it is to disarm satan. *Keep this in the forefront of your mind when an argument is likely.* satan is the instigator of all strife in relationships. He's behind every argument. Fight against him and not your loved one. They're not your enemy. You are just prey to satan's attempt at destroying the relationship. Forsake anger, pride, self-pity, bitterness, and all things that stem from unresolved conflicts. Not only are they products of the forces of evil listed in this verse, but, if not dealt with, they will become strongholds. And the aim is destruction. If you understand this and make a pact to fight the the *enemy of the relationship* together, it's only victory. If not, the enemy is refueled with every passing moment of discord. You have a choice to act and react as Jesus commands. Or you can choose the un-Godly way, furthering the strife—breaking down, rather than building up. You must forgive, and ask to be forgiven of your wrongs. If there's no resolution after you've done all you can to make things right, don't push the issue. You just have to let it go, and allow the Holy Spirit to work. Maintain Godliness, and keep your heart pure. Continue to battle for your loved one in prayer. Pray for a healing of their hurt. Pray against satan's influence. Release God's peace, patience, truth, and love. (*Be sure to read Ephesians 5–6. These chapters guide our relationships. It's no wonder this verse is placed here—to help *preserve* those relationships.)

Day 1: For our struggle is not against flesh and blood

Day 2: but against the rulers, against the powers

Day 3: For our struggle is not against flesh and blood, but against the rulers, against the powers

Day 4: against the world forces of this darkness

Day 5: but against the rulers, against the powers, against the world forces of this darkness

Day 6: For our struggle is not against flesh and blood, but against the rulers, against the powers, against the world forces of this darkness

(verse continued)

Tena Marchand

THOUGHTS, PRAYERS, AND TESTIMONIES

_____

_____

_____

_____

_____

_____

_____

_____

_____

_____

_____

_____

_____

_____

_____

_____

_____

_____

People are hurt when an offense wasn't intentional or even perceived as a wrong by the "offender"—and a lot of explaining just won't bring relief. You may not recall the events as recalled by them, but you can agree that there was some misunderstanding for which you can humble yourself and ask forgiveness. Acknowledge you weren't aware of hurting them, but you are sorry and you will try to avoid the same mistake. Once you've discussed it and you still think they have it wrong, leave it at that. You don't have to be right. They believe what they believe and it's truth to them—they're hurting by what they believe was an offense by you. In discussing your side of the issue, be careful not to get on the defensive. Keep an open heart before the Lord for any possible remembrance of some contributing factor to what their perception was. The only time to bring it up again is in the event that you clearly remember that there was wrong by you, and you need to make it right—but be careful not to rehash it into an argument again. Pray that satan no longer blind the eyes of you and your loved one. With all eyes open and all hearts obedient, there's a clear path to restoration. All will heal. But you must both be willing to die to self and let God rule. The whole process starts with just one person—let it be you.

Day 1: against the spiritual forces

Day 2: of wickedness in the heavenly places

Day 3: but against the rulers, against the powers, against the world forces of this darkness, against the spiritual forces of wickedness in the heavenly places.

Day 4: For our struggle is not against flesh and blood,

Day 5: but against the rulers, against the powers, against the world forces of this darkness, against the spiritual forces of wickedness in the heavenly places

Day 6: Ephesians 6:12 For our struggle is not against flesh and blood, but against the rulers, against the powers, against the world forces of this darkness, against the spiritual forces of wickedness in the heavenly places.

THOUGHTS, PRAYERS, AND TESTIMONIES

Isaiah 26:3 The steadfast of mind Thou wilt keep in perfect peace, because he trusts in Thee. (New King James Version: You will keep him in perfect peace, *whose mind is stayed on You*, because he trusts in You.)

A few years ago, I was experiencing a lot of stress for several weeks; and the impact of it affected my countenance. Ohhh, I didn't like that! I tried to keep myself at peace. As my sister and I were in worship one night, she had a word of knowledge from the Lord that I was doing exactly that—trying to manufacture peace myself. This verse became a re-call many times throughout my day. Then in an instant, without any anticipation, I felt the presence of the Person of Peace Himself saturate every bit of my being. There was total relaxation, starting from the top of my head, flowing right down to my feet. It was tangible. Peace is one of the fruit of the Holy Spirit, Who dwells in us. I found out that I could not create peace, no matter how hard I tried. I was trading the Person of Peace in me for my own efforts. I will guard against ever making such a mistake again. (Do note the last phrase in this scripture: "because he trusts in Thee." We need to cultivate trust in Him for all circumstances—it's the trust that makes for the peace.)

Day 1: The steadfast of mind

Day 2: Thou wilt keep

Day 3: The steadfast of mind Thou wilt keep

Day 4: in perfect peace

Day 5: The steadfast of mind Thou wilt keep in perfect peace

Day 6: because he trusts in Thee

Day 7: Isaiah 26:3 The steadfast of mind Thou wilt keep in perfect peace, because he trusts in Thee.

THOUGHTS, PRAYERS, AND TESTIMONIES

---

2 Corinthians 10:3–4 For though we walk in the flesh, we do not war according to the flesh, (4) for the weapons of our warfare are not of the flesh, but divinely powerful for the destruction of fortresses.

satan is always trying to trip us up with our human weaknesses. Left to ourselves, we are no match for anything in the spiritual world. We would have nothing with which to fight such a formidable enemy. But we have the Victor at our side. Actually, He lives in us.

I remember a conflict involving a very sensitive situation in which I had to hold fast to God's heart. There were many people on one side of the issue, and I alone on the other side. My only option was to stand in obedience to His Word. I remained quiet, entrusting every detail to Him. Then I realized that I was not alone—when we make decisions based on God's commands, that puts us on His side of any issue. Let Him lead. Follow Him closely with a loving heart toward those with whom you have opposing views. Keep the correct perspective of what the battle is all about in the spiritual world. Ephesians 6:12 says, "For our struggle is not against flesh and blood (human beings), but against the rulers, against the powers, against the world forces of this darkness, against the spiritual forces of wickedness in the Heavenly places." Every battle takes place there, where God and our Angels are fighting for us, as we obey His Word.

Day 1: For though we walk in the flesh

Day 2: we do not war according to the flesh

Day 3: For though we walk in the flesh, we do not war according to the flesh

Day 4: (4) for the weapons of our warfare

Day 5: are not of the flesh

Day 6: (4) for the weapons of our warfare are not of the flesh

Day 7: 2 Corinthians 10:3–4 For though we walk in the flesh, we do not war according to the flesh, (4) for the weapons of our warfare are not of the flesh

(verse continued)

Tena Marchand

THOUGHTS, PRAYERS, AND TESTIMONIES

_____

_____

_____

_____

_____

_____

_____

_____

_____

_____

_____

_____

_____

_____

_____

_____

_____

_____

Day 1: but divinely powerful

Day 2: For though we walk in the flesh, we do not war according to the flesh, (4) for the weapons of our warfare are not of the flesh, but divinely powerful

Day 3: for the destruction of fortresses

Day 4: but divinely powerful for the destruction of fortresses

Day 5: 2 Corinthians 10:3–4 For though we walk in the flesh, we do not war according to the flesh, (4) for the weapons of our warfare are not of the flesh, but divinely powerful for the destruction of fortresses.

THOUGHTS, PRAYERS, AND TESTIMONIES

2 Corinthians 10:5 We are destroying speculations and every lofty thing raised up against the knowledge of God, and we are taking every thought captive to the obedience of Christ,

It never hurts to repeat: every action and habit started with a thought. For example, many people are addicted to lustful thoughts and immorality. Perhaps it started by viewing improper bedroom scenes on television, or by seeing models skimpily clad in clothing catalogs. The addiction may even persist after a person has become a Christian. For those addicted to sexual immorality, counselors say that if a lustful thought is not dismissed within four to six seconds, the one being tempted will be caught! In 1 Corinthians 6:18, we are told to "flee" immorality. But we must flee any type of temptation: jealousy, gossip, pride, backbiting, lying, conceit—just to mention a few of our natural sinful ways. This fleeing is not a casual thing. It is escaping for safety, or life itself, just as one would flee a burning building. It is instant, not even prolonging itself for the four-to-six tragic seconds.

Our self-esteem is another area in which our thoughts can make an impact, even with a paralyzing effect. Most people have a very inferior concept of themselves in some way, that stifles not only their gifts and talents, but also their ease of expressing who they are. You can be set free from this by taking those negative thoughts captive to the obedience of Christ—for eternal destruction. See what God says about you and meditate on those thoughts.

Day 1: We are destroying speculations and every lofty thing

Day 2: raised up against the knowledge of God

Day 3: We are destroying speculations and every lofty thing raised up against the knowledge of God,

Day 4: and we are taking every thought captive

Day 5: to the obedience of Christ,

Day 6: and we are taking every thought captive to the obedience of Christ

Day 7: 2 Corinthians 10:5 We are destroying speculations and every lofty thing raised up against the knowledge of God, and we are taking every thought captive to the obedience of Christ

Take a few more days with this one, even another week, if needed. It's such an important scripture.

THOUGHTS, PRAYERS, AND TESTIMONIES

James 5:16 Therefore, confess your sins to one another, and pray for one another, so that you may be healed. The effective prayer of a righteous man can accomplish much.

When I confess my sins regarding attitudes towards others, it is usually dealt with between the Lord and myself. But there were a couple of situations in which I just could not shake the sin of my thoughts. In one instance, I was offended by a roommate. Although I took the right action, my inner attitude was not right. I could not free myself of a little resentment toward her, neither in heart nor mind. Finally, after reading this verse, I confessed my wrong to another sister in the Lord. To my surprise, I was completely set free at that very moment! There was never again a battle with that situation. If you do not get the victory in due time and are in danger of a fixed sinful attitude, carry the burden to another non-gossipy, *trusted* believer.

Day 1: Therefore, confess your sins to one another

Day 2: and pray for one another

Day 3: Therefore, confess your sins to one another, and pray for one another,

Day 4: so that you may be healed.

Day 5: Therefore, confess your sins to one another, and pray for one another, so that you may be healed.

(verse continued)

TENA MARCHAND

THOUGHTS, PRAYERS, AND TESTIMONIES

_____

_____

_____

_____

_____

_____

_____

_____

_____

_____

_____

_____

_____

_____

_____

_____

_____

_____

Day 1: The effective prayer of a righteous man

Day 2: can accomplish much.

Day 3: The effective prayer of a righteous man can accomplish much.

Day 4: James 5:16 Therefore, confess your sins to one another, and pray for one another, so that you may be healed. The effective prayer of a righteous man can accomplish much.

THOUGHTS, PRAYERS, AND TESTIMONIES

_____

_____

_____

_____

_____

_____

_____

_____

_____

_____

_____

_____

_____

_____

_____

_____

Mark 11:25 And whenever you stand praying, forgive, if you have anything against anyone; so that your Father also Who is in Heaven may forgive you your transgressions.

Never, for any reason, are we exempt from forgiving anyone who offended us. Jesus paid a high price for their forgiveness and it must be extended to them by us as well. This can be very difficult sometimes. Perhaps you should focus on the Cross and all He went through for you in your offenses. Had you been the only person on this earth, He would have still gone through all the brutality and ultimate death offered for your forgiveness. And He was blameless! What we suffer on this earth at the offense of others does not compare to what He suffered—for us. Keep on forgiving, no matter what you feel. As you are faithful to fight your attitude and yield to His Spirit, God will grace you with the removal of the hard feelings. It will become your lifestyle to honestly forgive future offenses immediately, giving the enemy no opportunity to instill any emotions or attitudes that may lead to bitterness.

Day 1: And whenever you stand praying,

Day 2: forgive, if you have anything against anyone

Day 3: And whenever you stand praying, forgive, if you have anything against anyone;

Day 4: so that your Father also Who is in Heaven

Day 5: may forgive you your transgressions.

Day 6: so that your Father also Who is in Heaven may forgive you your transgressions.

Day 7: Mark 11:25 And whenever you stand praying, forgive, if you have anything against anyone; so that your Father also Who is in Heaven may forgive you your transgressions.

THOUGHTS, PRAYERS, AND TESTIMONIES

_____

_____

_____

_____

_____

_____

_____

_____

_____

_____

_____

_____

_____

_____

_____

_____

_____

Mark 11:26 But if you do not forgive, neither will your Father Who is in Heaven forgive your transgressions.

God wants us all to receive our forgiveness. It is equally important to Him that we forgive others—otherwise He will not forgive us. Imagine the heart that readily receives His forgiveness, and at the same time refuses to forgive others. There's just something wrong with that picture. *Repeat failure is <u>not</u> the problem, but a lack of <u>trying</u> to forgive.* In your honest attempts, you are beautiful. When you find it hard to forgive, ask for God's grace to help you. Just say, "I can't, but You can in me, Lord." And He will. Be faithful. He will eventually remove the pain and emotions from the memories, rendering them powerless over you.

*Be careful not to rely on your own efforts to fight off anger and bitterness—you will be convinced that it's impossible and end up justifying yourself. You've got to let God help you. Get scriptures that will guide your thoughts and heal your heart. Keep confessing the right attitude to God, no matter what you feel. When satan stirs up your emotions again, don't entertain the memories. They invade your mind with a force that's very difficult to stop, and you're quickly trapped. Resist letting the past fill your heart. Immediately say, "No." Let God fill you with the things of Himself, leaving no room for satan's assault. You will allow one or the other to occupy your mind. Let God have that place. Routinely read His Word, which is how you interact with Him. Turn your thoughts to His goodness. Pray for those involved. As you are faithful, He will heal you and set you free.

Day 1: But if you do not forgive,

Day 2: neither will your Father Who is in Heaven

Day 3: But if you do not forgive, neither will your Father Who is in Heaven

Day 4: forgive your transgressions

Day 5: Mark 11:26 But if you do not forgive, neither will your Father Who is in Heaven forgive your transgressions

Day 6: Mark 11:25–26 And whenever you stand praying, forgive, if you have anything against anyone; so that your Father also Who is in Heaven may forgive you your transgressions. (26) But if you do not forgive, neither will your Father Who is in Heaven forgive your transgressions.

THOUGHTS, PRAYERS, AND TESTIMONIES

_____

_____

_____

_____

_____

_____

_____

_____

_____

_____

_____

_____

_____

_____

_____

_____

Matthew 21:21–22 And Jesus answered and said to them, "Truly I say to you, if you have faith, and do not doubt, you shall not only do what was done to the fig tree, but even if you say to this mountain, 'Be taken up and cast into the sea,' it shall happen. (22) And all things you ask in prayer, believing, you shall receive." (Mark 11:23 says, "...*and does not doubt in his heart*, but believes that what he says is going to happen, it shall be granted him.")

When exercising faith, you may have to battle satan-inflicted thoughts that try to seize what you believe in your heart. satan knows that our faith can move mountains and make the impossible things possible. Consequently, this savage is relentless in his attempts to destroy your faith—and it's felt. Imagine holding a shield up with a very large object being thrown at it. You feel the jolt, maybe even uncomfortably, but there's no damage to the shield. Doubt is hurled at you that way, but your faith needn't be affected. You, too, can be relentless in the battle. Just continue to give credence to what you believe in your heart. It's what you believe there that rules. The mind has been referred to as the "doubt box." Don't permit it to overrule your heart's belief—you must saturate your mind with the scriptures to make the things of your heart solid. Meditate on the appropriate opposing scriptures to any doubts that defy your faith. You will build it to the extent that satan will tire of your persistence; and he will leave—defeated by your unshakable faith. (The disciples were told to speak to the mountain. Speak your faith into action.)

Day 1: And Jesus answered and said to them,

Day 2: "Truly I say to you,

Day 3: And Jesus answered and said to them, "Truly I say to you

Day 4: if you have faith, and do not doubt,

Day 5: And Jesus answered and said to them, "Truly I say to you, if you have faith, and do not doubt,

Day 6: you shall not only do what was done to the fig tree,

Day 7: but even if you say to this mountain,

(verse continued)

Tena Marchand

THOUGHTS, PRAYERS, AND TESTIMONIES

_____

_____

_____

_____

_____

_____

_____

_____

_____

_____

_____

_____

_____

_____

_____

_____

_____

_____

I live in an area of the country where hurricanes are common. They are powerful enough to uproot huge trees, and do extensive damage to large buildings, reducing them to rubble in seconds. But they do not move mountains. Jesus says that your faith can. He offered the disciples the miracle of *telling* the mountain to be taken up and cast into the sea. If this were to be done physically, the hard part would be taking up the mountain—the hard part in our desperate trials is building our faith for a miracle. Once the mountain's thrown into the sea, momentum takes it from there—the easy part. Once your faith activates the miracle, it's all by an effortless supernatural act of God—the easy part.

Day 1: you shall not only do what was done to the fig tree, but even if you say to this mountain

Day 2: 'Be taken up and cast into the sea,' it shall happen.

Day 3: you shall not only do what was done to the fig tree, but even if you say to this mountain 'Be taken up and cast into the sea,' it shall happen.

Day 4: (22) "And all things you ask in prayer,

Day 5: believing, you shall receive."

Day 6: (22) "And all things you ask in prayer, believing, you shall receive."

Day 7: Matthew 21:21–22 And Jesus answered and said to them, "Truly I say to you, if you have faith, and do not doubt, you shall not only do what was done to the fig tree, but even if you say to this mountain, 'Be taken up and cast into the sea,' it shall happen." (22) "And all things you ask in prayer, believing, you shall receive."

THOUGHTS, PRAYERS, AND TESTIMONIES

Ephesians 4:32 And be kind to one another, tender-hearted, forgiving each other, just as God in Christ also has forgiven you.

Years ago I had a roommate with whom I had a hard time within my heart for some reason. I struggled with my un-Godly attitude. When I saw this verse, I asked the Lord to give me a tender heart for her. Shortly after this, we were climbing the stairs of a church. She was a few steps ahead of me. Why in Heaven, I do not know, but the appearance of her little ankles just broke my heart! A tenderness and compassion overtook me. Since that day, I was freed from the unexplained struggles. God wants to honor prayers that allow His love to operate in us. We, ourselves, can not manufacture that perfect love. But all that we need is present in us, because He is in us. Ask God to grace you with whatever you need of love's virtues.

Day 1: And be kind to one another

Day 2: tender-hearted, forgiving each other,

Day 3: And be kind to one another, tender-hearted, forgiving each other

Day 4: just as God in Christ also has forgiven you.

Day 5: Ephesians 4:32 And be kind to one another, tender-hearted, forgiving each other, just as God in Christ also has forgiven you.

THOUGHTS, PRAYERS, AND TESTIMONIES

_____

_____

_____

_____

_____

_____

_____

_____

_____

_____

_____

_____

_____

_____

_____

_____

_____

John 10:10 The thief comes only to steal, and kill, and destroy; I came that they might have life, and might have it abundantly.

We have to know what's operating out there. satan is a thief, and thieves take what is not theirs—he takes what *belongs* to us. All that we have need of is in the Name of Jesus. Stand up for what's yours in relationships, health, finances, and everything else. satan wants to steal, kill, and destroy. This is what he is all about. He comes ONLY to steal, kill, and destroy. Thieves are to be caught, prosecuted, and maybe even jailed. They are to stop stealing and return what they stole. So, too, with satan. Put him in his place. Jesus provides abundance. That is far more than we need, but we shouldn't let the enemy take it or hold back any measure of what is meant to be ours.

Day 1: The thief comes only to steal,

Day 2: and kill, and destroy;

Day 3: The thief comes only to steal, and kill, and destroy

Day 4: I came that they might have life,

Day 5: and might have it abundantly.

Day 6: I came that they might have life, and might have it abundantly.

Day 7: John 10:10 The thief comes only to steal, and kill, and destroy; I came that they might have life, and might have it abundantly.

THOUGHTS, PRAYERS, AND TESTIMONIES

Proverbs 3:5–6 Trust in the LORD with all your heart, and do not lean on your own understanding. (6) In all your ways acknowledge Him, and He will make your paths straight.

As a brand new believer, this was the first scripture that really ministered to me. I was dating someone who led me to the Lord, but was not himself committed to God. Fairly soon, I learned that a believer and non-believer should not marry, so I broke up with him—painfully. I remember torturing myself with the thought, "If he finds someone else and I'm hurting, it will be my own fault, because I broke up with him." The instant I read this verse, it gave me the greatest peace! He has my life planned out and I can certainly trust His every decision. I was rescued from my own understanding, which had the potential to lead to wrong choices. The decision to break up was based on His commands and guidance. How could I go wrong?

Day 1: Trust in the LORD with all your heart,

Day 2: And do not lean on your own understanding.

Day 3: Trust in the LORD with all your heart, and do not lean on your own understanding.

Day 4: (6) In all your ways acknowledge Him,

Day 5: Trust in the LORD with all your heart, and do not lean on your own understanding. (6) In all your ways acknowledge Him

Day 6: and He will make your paths straight.

Day 7: Proverbs 3:5–6 Trust in the LORD with all your heart, and do not lean on your own understanding. (6) In all your ways acknowledge Him, and He will make your paths straight.

THOUGHTS, PRAYERS, AND TESTIMONIES

_____

_____

_____

_____

_____

_____

_____

_____

_____

_____

_____

_____

_____

_____

_____

_____

_____

1 John 4:18 There is no fear in love; but perfect love casts out fear, because fear involves punishment, and the one who fears is not perfected in love. (Note: Greek translation of "punishment" is "punishment; *torment*".)

God is so good. So many times in my daily reading, the particular passages were appropriate and perfect for the need of the moment. There was no need for a word search on any topic—my loving Father had His counsel ready. In my Christian circle, there was a newcomer who started dating the guy with whom I had just terminated a relationship. I did NOT want to meet her and inflict pain upon myself. I avoided any possibility of an encounter with her, and *tormented* myself with the thought of how painful it would be. But we all three lived next to each other, attended the same church, and had the same friends. It was inevitable that we would meet. In that time frame, this verse was a life-changing revelation for me. I realized that as a Christian, I must demonstrate perfect love toward her. There's a very fine line between perfect love and the torment we experience. Clearly, I was standing in fear, which produced a lot of imagination that resulted in self-inflicted torment. Perfect love casts out fear. I decided to cross that fine line and befriend her—and guess what? The perfect love immediately buffered all pain; and the fear and torment vanished! We became very good friends.

Day 1: There is no fear in love

Day 2: but perfect love casts out fear

Day 3: There is no fear in love; but perfect love casts out fear

Day 4: because fear involves punishment

Day 5: There is no fear in love; but perfect love casts out fear, because fear involves punishment,

Day 6: and the one who fears is not perfected in love.

Day 7: 1 John 4:18 There is no fear in love; but perfect love casts out fear, because fear involves punishment, and the one who fears is not perfected in love.

THOUGHTS, PRAYERS, AND TESTIMONIES

Hebrews 12:1 Therefore, since we have so great a cloud of witnesses surrounding us, let us also lay aside every encumbrance, and the sin which so easily entangles us, and let us run with endurance the race that is set before us,

As we read the Bible, there's so much we can learn from the faith of those who have gone before us. I moved out of state for one and a half years to test the six-year off-and-on relationship with my first boyfriend—would the distance make it or break it? After that time, he ended it while I had other expectations. I was left hurting. I had just moved back to my very small hometown to get to know Daddy better and attend nursing school. With the broken relationship, loss of my church and friends, a now limited social life, and no possibility of a husband there, I felt that all was taken from me—no comparison to the magnitude of Job's losses, but I felt I identified with him. For consolation, I read that book of the Bible. In the first chapter, God asked satan if he considered Job (for trials), and said that there was no one like him. He was blameless and upright, fearing God, and turning away from evil. satan challenged that if all were taken from him, Job would turn from God. satan was then permitted access to all of his possessions—children, crops, livestock, health—but not his very life. When I read this, I felt that God was trusting *me* to stand for *Him*. "Take what you will from Tena. She will remain faithful to Me." I was so blessed and full of joy by the thought that He believed in my faithfulness to Him! That alone lifted almost all the pain. Through it all, God said that Job never sinned, in spite of his multiple losses. His example helped me to lay aside self-pity, which could've led to anger and bitterness.

Day 1: Therefore, since we have so great

Day 2: a cloud of witnesses surrounding us

Day 3: Therefore, since we have so great a cloud of witnesses surrounding us

Day 4: let us also lay aside every encumbrance

Day 5: Therefore, since we have so great a cloud of witnesses surrounding us, let us also lay aside every encumbrance

Day 6: and the sin which so easily entangles us,

(verse continued)

TENA MARCHAND

THOUGHTS, PRAYERS, AND TESTIMONIES

Day 1: Therefore, since we have so great a cloud of witnesses surrounding us, let us also lay aside every encumbrance, and the sin which so easily entangles us

Day 2: let us also lay aside every encumbrance,

Day 3: let us also lay aside every encumbrance, and the sin which so easily entangles us

Day 4: and let us run with endurance

Day 5: the race that is set before us,

Day 6: and let us run with endurance the race that is set before us,

Day 7: Hebrews 12:1 Therefore, since we have so great a cloud of witnesses surrounding us, let us also lay aside every encumbrance, and the sin which so easily entangles us, and let us run with endurance the race that is set before us,

THOUGHTS, PRAYERS, AND TESTIMONIES

_____

_____

_____

_____

_____

_____

_____

_____

_____

_____

_____

_____

_____

_____

_____

_____

_____

_____

Hebrews 12:2 fixing our eyes on Jesus, the author and perfecter of faith, Who for the joy set before Him endured the cross, despising the shame, and has sat down at the right hand of the throne of God.

We talk about "taking up our cross"—the process of "dying to self" when going through trials or giving up selfish ways. But in spite of some accomplishments, we may be harboring some wrong attitudes, for example, as we experience conflict with others. In the journey, we may have acted or reacted contrary to His ways. We may have focused more on our self-justification than on trying to maintain true Godliness toward the other person. Our journey *to* the Cross is just as important as "our death" *on* the Cross. Jesus was spit upon, humiliated, mocked, hated, abused, tormented, and brutally beaten for us. Yet, He continued to love every one of His offenders along His path to Golgotha, where He was nailed to the Cross—for their sins, and ours as well. How easy it would have been to hate back. But, had He violated any of the virtues of love during His journey to the Cross, His death on the Cross would have been of no effect. It would all have been in vain. To endure, Jesus kept His eyes on the "joy" set before Him—pleasing the Father by making a way for us to go to Heaven; defeating satan; and providing victory for us in every situation. We must keep our focus on Jesus through all trials, following His example. He will give as much grace as we need.

Day 1: fixing our eyes on Jesus,

Day 2: the author and perfecter of faith.

Day 3: fixing our eyes on Jesus, the author and perfecter of faith,

Day 4: Who for the joy set before Him

Day 5: fixing our eyes on Jesus, the author and perfecter of faith, Who for the joy set before Him

Day 6: endured the cross, despising the shame,

Day 7: Who for the joy set before Him endured the cross, despising the shame,

(verse continued)

TENA MARCHAND

THOUGHTS, PRAYERS, AND TESTIMONIES

_____

_____

_____

_____

_____

_____

_____

_____

_____

_____

_____

_____

_____

_____

_____

_____

_____

_____

_____

Day 1: fixing our eyes on Jesus, the author and perfecter of faith, Who for the joy set before Him endured the cross, despising the shame

Day 2: and has sat down at the right hand

Day 3: of the throne of God.

Day 4: and has sat down at the right hand of the throne of God.

Day 5: Who for the joy set before Him endured the cross, despising the shame

Day 6: Who for the joy set before Him endured the cross, despising the shame, and has sat down at the right hand of the throne of God.

Day 7: Hebrews 12:2 fixing our eyes on Jesus, the author and perfecter of faith, Who for the joy set before Him endured the cross, despising the shame, and has sat down at the right hand of the throne of God.

THOUGHTS, PRAYERS, AND TESTIMONIES

_____

_____

_____

_____

_____

_____

_____

_____

_____

_____

_____

_____

_____

_____

_____

_____

_____

_____

Hebrews 12:11 All discipline for the moment seems not to be joyful, but sorrowful; yet to those who have been trained by it, afterwards it yields the peaceful fruit of righteousness.

Parents know the importance of disciplining their children. When one of my nieces, Joy, was three years old, and had just experienced a little disciplinary training by her mom, she came to me for "comfort." After she related the story to me, I asked her who was right—she or her mom. Her answer? "Mama." Always with reaffirmation of love, this little one was consistently disciplined when needed. As a result, she was learning right from wrong. And she was able to concede that Mama was right! Through the years, I have experienced repetitive defeat in thought, word, and deed. We know that God gives us the way of escape from temptations (1 Corinthians 10:5, earlier memory verse) by using scripture to resist satan. That is the easy way out—submitting to His Word and using it against the enemy. But when I was not willing to let go, He would at some point allow a discomfort that really got my attention. And that was mercy! I pushed God to more drastic measures to help me overcome a habit that should have been forsaken long before that measure of discipline was needed. The peaceful fruit of righteousness resulted. God is good.

Day 1: All discipline for the moment

Day 2: seems not to be joyful, but sorrowful;

Day 3: All discipline for the moment seems not to be joyful, but sorrowful

Day 4: yet to those who have been trained by it

Day 5: All discipline for the moment seems not to be joyful, but sorrowful; yet to those who have been trained by it

Day 6: afterwards it yields the peaceful fruit of righteousness.

Day 7: Hebrews 12:11 All discipline for the moment seems not to be joyful, but sorrowful; yet to those who have been trained by it, afterwards it yields the peaceful fruit of righteousness.

THOUGHTS, PRAYERS, AND TESTIMONIES

Philippians 3:13 Brethren, I do not regard myself as having laid hold of it yet; but one thing I do: forgetting what lies behind and reaching forward to what lies ahead,

We are in a perpetual state of "not having laid hold of it yet." We always have something for which to strive—becoming more like Jesus and fulfilling His plans for our lives. The past can paralyze our present and future; and we tend to accommodate ourselves to the way things have always been. Mistakes and failures, regrets, and feelings of guilt all serve to discourage us. Don't stay there, thinking things will never change. God can, and will indeed, transform you. He always intended freedom with great things for you (John 8:36). Cooperate with Him. Make a concerted effort to leave the past behind and go forward. Get in step with what God has planned for you.

For a couple of years, I had been pleading for God's grace and peace in a challenging area. (When your need is intense, you plead. Actually, I was begging!) When I reached absolute rock bottom, I could have been incapacitated. But I said, "Tomorrow you will see a new woman." To my utter amazement, it happened—overnight! It was no less than a miracle. For the next few months, I faced challenge after challenge. There was no pressure whatsoever, and there was fluid movement all day long. I was filled with the joy of God's goodness to deliver me from two to three years of what "had always been." Whatever your challenge is, keep on believing for God to rescue you. In due time, He will. (If you have a relapse, it's not the end. I've been there, too. satan is always looking for the opportunity to generate setbacks in your life. Be wise and alert to his evil schemes. Rest assured that God is in control, and that He has His purposes in everything. Increase your faith in Him and stay strong—you will overcome again.)

Day 1: Brethren, I do not regard myself

Day 2: as having laid hold of it yet

Day 3: Brethren, I do not regard myself as having laid hold of it yet

Day 4: but one thing I do:

Day 5: but one thing I do: forgetting what lies behind

Day 6: and reaching forward to what lies ahead,

Day 7: Philippians 3:13 Brethren, I do not regard myself as having laid hold of it yet; but one thing I do: forgetting what lies behind and reaching forward to what lies ahead,

THOUGHTS, PRAYERS, AND TESTIMONIES

_____

_____

_____

_____

_____

_____

_____

_____

_____

_____

_____

_____

_____

_____

_____

_____

_____

_____

Philippians 3:14 I press on toward the goal for the prize of the upward call of God in Christ Jesus.

Ohhhh. Our overall goal for which to strive is entrance into Heaven—our prize for enduring to the end. When we have this as our utmost goal and put all our effort into it, all else falls into place. It's not so much a *work of self*, but a strong desire to please Him and allow Him to live through you, that *requires* work. When someone runs a race to win, he does everything to keep himself fit and ready. He doesn't get on a different track, nor can he run two races at one time. He must not allow any distractions. The only way to win is by keeping his eyes on the finish mark and to keep running towards it. The serious runner will consistently train, while eating right, and getting plenty of fluids and proper rest. He will abstain from anything that will cause him to lose the race.

For years I ran two to three miles every day. I did everything right. The more I ran, the more I desired to run. It naturally encouraged the right diet, rest, and good habits. I never did anything to hinder my health or performance. The more I focused my efforts, the more all the right habits intensified and perpetuated itself. Our relationship and faithfulness to God will grow stronger and stronger as we consistently keep our focus on Him and obey his Word. (This week we will add the previous week's verse as well.)

Day 1: (14) I press on toward the goal

Day 2: for the prize of the upward call

Day 3: (14) I press on toward the goal for the prize of the upward call

Day 4: 13–14 Brethren, I do not regard myself as having laid hold of it yet; but one thing I do: forgetting what lies behind and reaching forward to what lies ahead, (14) I press on toward the goal for the prize of the upward call

Day 5: (14) I press on toward the goal for the prize of the upward call of God in Christ Jesus.

Day 6: Philippians 3:13–14 Brethren, I do not regard myself as having laid hold of it yet; but one thing I do: forgetting what lies behind and reaching forward to what lies ahead, (14) I press on toward the goal for the prize of the upward call of God in Christ Jesus.

THOUGHTS, PRAYERS, AND TESTIMONIES

_____

_____

_____

_____

_____

_____

_____

_____

_____

_____

_____

_____

_____

_____

_____

_____

_____

_____

Proverbs 23:7 For as he thinks within himself, so he is. (KJV "As a man thinketh within his heart...")

Our thoughts cut right into our hearts, splitting it wide open to root who we are. They are the stronghold of our emotions and passions, the constant activity of our mind, and the ruling power over our will and character—the control of the very life of us. Unfortunately, our thoughts are largely against us through feelings of inadequacy, failures, fears, shyness, criticism, and various other hindrances. We can't imagine change, so we settle for the way we are. But God supplies grace for us to overcome ALL negatives and ALL strongholds. It's all in how we choose to think. I have memorized certain scriptures before, quoting them over and over again, until I reaped the benefit of transformation in favor of the scripture. It became my new thought and a new me. Living the scripture even became effortless. I was transformed by His Word. It is nothing of self, but all of His life in you.

Day 1: For as he thinks within himself

Day 2: Proverbs 23:7 For as he thinks within himself, so he is.

THOUGHTS, PRAYERS, AND TESTIMONIES

_____

_____

_____

_____

_____

_____

_____

_____

_____

_____

_____

_____

_____

_____

_____

_____

_____

_____

Matthew 24:13 But the one who endures to the end, he shall be saved.

Dear Fellow Christian, be ever so careful not to let anything pull your heart away from the Lord. In verse thirteen of the Parable of the Seeds (Luke 8:9–15), Jesus explained the falling away of one of the four seeds: "And those on the rocky soil are those who, when they hear, receive the Word with joy; and these have no firm root; they believe for a while, and in time of temptation fall away." This cannot be more clear. This person got saved and then fell away. Some Christians might backslide and come back into their relationship with God, but there are those who leave and never come back. Let this verse be the theme of your heart, the thrust of your race for the upward call to Heaven, and the very thing that seals your commitment to Christ. We never know when our very own personal lives will end. We must always be ready to meet Him face to face—at the Judgment Seat.

Day 1: But the one who endures to the end,

Day 2: he shall be saved.

Day 3: Matthew 24:13 But the one who endures to the end, he shall be saved.

THOUGHTS, PRAYERS, AND TESTIMONIES

1 John 1:9-10 If we confess our sins, He is faithful and righteous to forgive us our sins and to cleanse us from all unrighteousness. (10) If we say that we have not sinned, we make Him a liar, and His Word is not in us.

I used to think that when we confessed our sins, God gave us a clean slate and we started fresh. But it's more than that. As I studied this verse, I realized it means, yes, (1) We do get a clean slate. (2) In confessing our sins, we are expected to straighten out, but we are not left on our own to do so. The Holy Spirit is a part of it all. He will help us. Then to top it all off, it also includes (3) Removing the consequences of our sin—to the point that if sickness were a consequence, God loves us enough to heal us!

Day 1: If we confess our sins

Day 2: He is faithful and righteous

Day 3: If we confess our sins, He is faithful and righteous

Day 4: to forgive us our sins

Day 5: and to cleanse us from all unrighteousness

Day 6: to forgive us our sins and to cleanse us from all unrighteousness

Day 7: 1 John 1:9 If we confess our sins, He is faithful and righteous to forgive us our sins and to cleanse us from all unrighteousness

(verse continued)

TENA MARCHAND

THOUGHTS, PRAYERS, AND TESTIMONIES

_____

_____

_____

_____

_____

_____

_____

_____

_____

_____

_____

_____

_____

_____

_____

_____

_____

_____

_____

(10) If we say that we have not sinned, we make Him a liar, and His Word is not in us.

We get nowhere if we do not confess our sins. It even blocks His presence and answers to prayer. Because of pride, I used to have difficulty owning up to my wrongs. Pride does not feel good—do not give that nasty thing a place in your life. Forsake your concern for what others think. We need to be pleasing to the Father, and being in agreement with Him about our sin pleases Him. It's a pure heart, and it offers a new sense of freedom.

As I matured in my relationship with Jesus, it became easier to be honest and transparent. Admitting to the truth often involves humiliation; but when you strive to please Him, it always has a beautiful result. Humility is one of the most touching, and again beautiful, reflections of Jesus in a person's life. It's a great witness and work of God.

Day 1: If we say that we have not sinned

Day 2: we make Him a liar

Day 3: If we say that we have not sinned, we make Him a liar

Day 4: and His Word is not in us.

Day 5: If we say that we have not sinned, we make Him a liar, and His Word is not in us.

Day 6: 1 John 1:9-10 If we confess our sins, He is faithful and righteous to forgive us our sins and to cleanse us from all unrighteousness. (10) If we say that we have not sinned, we make Him a liar, and His Word is not in us.

THOUGHTS, PRAYERS, AND TESTIMONIES

Gal 2:20 I have been crucified with Christ; and it is no longer I who live, but Christ lives in me; and the life which I now live in the flesh I live by faith in the Son of God, Who loved me, and delivered Himself up for me.

This verse became the anchor for one of my sisters in her devotion to Jesus—I was always astonished by its manifestation. In her latter years, she consistently gave God His place to live through her. In the hardest of trials, she especially relinquished all rights to self. She was very focused on His perspective. I can still hear her saying, "I've got the fear of God in me!" Then she would quote this verse. She was a very beautiful example of Christ crucified. After going through five to six months of terminal sickness, she died. She had the absolute sweetest countenance. With her eyes closed, I could still see a twinkle at the outer corners of her eyes.

Day 1: I have been crucified with Christ

Day 2: and it is no longer I who live,

Day 3: I have been crucified with Christ; and it is no longer I who live

Day 4: but Christ lives in me

Day 5: I have been crucified with Christ; and it is no longer I who live, but Christ lives in me

(verse continued)

Tena Marchand

THOUGHTS, PRAYERS, AND TESTIMONIES

_____

_____

_____

_____

_____

_____

_____

_____

_____

_____

_____

_____

_____

_____

_____

_____

Day 1: and the life which I now live in the flesh

Day 2: I live by faith in the Son of God

Day 3: and the life which I now live in the flesh I live by faith in the Son of God

Day 4: I have been crucified with Christ; and it is no longer I who live, but Christ lives in me and the life which I now live in the flesh I live by faith in the Son of God

Day 5: Who loved me, and delivered Himself up for me.

Day 6: Galatians 2:20 I have been crucified with Christ; and it is no longer I who live, but Christ lives in me; and the life which I now live in the flesh I live by faith in the Son of God, Who loved me, and delivered Himself up for me.

THOUGHTS, PRAYERS, AND TESTIMONIES

Psalms 103:20 Bless the LORD, you His Angels, mighty in strength, who perform His Word, obeying the voice of His Word!

For as long as I can remember, my mother has always dispatched the Angels. To this day, at eighty-seven years old, she is still faithful to do so. I heard a well-known Christian Bible teacher, Marilyn Hickey, teaching on Angels. She said there are guardian Angels appointed to believers. She believes "some are very bored with the believers to whom they are appointed because Psalms 103:20 says that Angels move at the command of His Word. So when we speak God's Word, it activates Angels. But believers who never speak the promises of God give their Angels nothing to do, because they are not given the Word to activate them." I also heard a brother to whom God gave many revelations about Angels. He said that there are Angels assigned for EVERY need—relationships, finances, health, safety, etc. Without Jesus, none of this would be possible. He was gracious enough to assign Angels to each one of us. Speak and pray God's Word on any subject to enable the Angels to move on your behalf.

Day 1: Bless the LORD, you His Angels,

Day 2: mighty in strength,

Day 3: Bless the LORD, you His Angels, mighty in strength

Day 4: who perform His Word,

Day 5: obeying the voice of His Word!

Day 6: who perform His Word, obeying the voice of His Word!

Day 7: Psalms 103:20 Bless the LORD, you His Angels, mighty in strength, who perform His Word, obeying the voice of His Word!

THOUGHTS, PRAYERS, AND TESTIMONIES

_____

_____

_____

_____

_____

_____

_____

_____

_____

_____

_____

_____

_____

_____

_____

_____

_____

_____

_____

_____

Matthew 18:10 See that you do not despise one of these little ones, for I say to you, that their Angels in Heaven continually behold the face of My Father Who is in Heaven.

Over a span of nineteen years, I've been telling a couple of my nieces that God gave them Angels for their birthdays when they were born. It seems one of these babies reached her twenties overnight. Out of curiosity, I asked her all those years later, "What did Jesus give you for your birthday?" Her answer was quick and spontaneous, "Angels." It is my daily prayer that all the little ones know Jesus at an early age, and that they know how to call on His Name for their Angels to be dispatched—that they would be quick, active, and victorious in time of need. I can just see them standing at full attention, very focused on God, ready to hasten to the aide of a child. They are assigned to us for life; no matter how old we get, our Angels will always be at our disposal.

Day 1: See that you do not despise one of these little ones

Day 2: for I say to you,

Day 3: that their Angels in Heaven

Day 4: for I say to you, that their Angels in Heaven

Day 5: See that you do not despise one of these little ones, for I say to you, that their Angels in Heaven

Day 6: continually behold the face of My Father Who is in Heaven.

Day 7: Matthew 18:10 See that you do not despise one of these little ones, for I say to you, that their Angels in Heaven continually behold the face of My Father Who is in Heaven.

THOUGHTS, PRAYERS, AND TESTIMONIES

_____

_____

_____

_____

_____

_____

_____

_____

_____

_____

_____

_____

_____

_____

_____

_____

_____

Psalms 91:10-11 No evil will befall you, nor will any plague come near your tent. (11) For He will give His Angels charge concerning you, to guard you in all your ways.

I had been telling my great niece, Jordan, about her Angels since she was just months old. When she was two, she and her family were at my house for part of the Christmas season. One of the gifts I gave her was a book about Angels. As soon as we finished opening gifts, we read the book. She then looked at different places in the room, saying she saw an Angel over there and then another in a different place. She had a fixed gaze for several seconds in each area, where there was nothing to catch your attention. One place was in the pitch of the cathedral ceiling above a large bookcase. I believe with all my heart that she actually saw them. The following day, we were visiting at my sister's home. I asked Jordan to tell her where the Angels are—thinking she would say, "All around me." But she said, "At Teno's!" This added to my already solid belief that she saw them. They are always watching over us, ready to intervene on our behalf. Days later, when her mom asked her what the Angels looked like, she described them all differently, and was still saying they were "at Teno's."

(I have three consecutive scriptures on Angels. Please be careful not to put any emphasis and trust in them over Jesus. Anything we put above Him is an idol, even though it's not our recognition or intention at all. Angels are wonderful and powerful ministering spirits that God has assigned to each one of us. They move in obedience to His Word. Just as it's only through Jesus that we can enter Heaven, it's only in His Name that we can pray to God the Father—not through or to Angels, Mary, or saints; not to Buddah, Allah, or any being other than the one true God. I was in error until I started reading the Bible.)

Day 1: No evil will befall you

Day 2: nor will any plague come near your tent

Day 3: No evil will befall you, nor will any plague come near your tent

Day 4: For He will give His Angels concerning you

Day 5: No evil will befall you, nor will any plague come near your tent. (11) For He will give His Angels charge concerning you

Day 6: to guard you in all your ways.

Day 7: Psalms 91:10-11 No evil will befall you, nor will any plague come near your tent. (11) For He will give His Angels charge concerning you, to guard you in all your ways.

THOUGHTS, PRAYERS, AND TESTIMONIES

Psalms 4:8 In peace I will both lie down and sleep, for Thou alone, O LORD, dost make me to dwell in safety.

Several years ago, I lived in a large trailer park. One July 4, there was a worker from the electrical company reading meters. My family and I noticed him at the back end of my mobile home just as they were leaving from a late afternoon visit. Because it was a holiday and we weren't able to verify who he was by uniform or workplace badge, we were a little skeptical of his presence. (Bless his heart—I'm sure he recognized our quiet scrutiny and suspicion, and felt very uncomfortable himself.) At bedtime, my scary-cat imagination went right back to this person. Now gripped with fear, I decided to sleep in the center of the house (kitchen floor!) for an awareness of any possible sounds from one end of the house to the other. When I began reading my Bible, I immediately came across Psalms127:1, "Unless the Lord guards the city, the watchman keeps awake in vain." Who was I to try to stay alert and on-guard to anything in the night? It was up to the Lord to guard me—His Word settled it for me. I closed my Bible and drifted off into peaceful sleep. God directed me to that scripture to assure me of His protection. (Thank You, Lord!)

Day 1: In peace I will

Day 2: both lie down and sleep

Day 3: In peace I will both lie down and sleep

Day 4: for Thou alone, O LORD

Day 5: dost make me to dwell in safety

Day 6: for Thou alone, O LORD, dost make me to dwell in safety.

Day 7: Psalms 4:8 In peace I will both lie down and sleep, for Thou alone, O LORD, dost make me to dwell in safety.

THOUGHTS, PRAYERS, AND TESTIMONIES

_____

_____

_____

_____

_____

_____

_____

_____

_____

_____

_____

_____

_____

_____

_____

_____

_____

Philippians 2:14–15 Do all things without grumbling or disputing; (15) that you may prove yourselves to be blameless and innocent, children of God above reproach in the midst of a crooked and perverse generation, among whom you appear as lights in the world,

As Christians, we must be mindful of how we represent God. In all of our encounters, we must give Him place as Master, to the point that He can say, "Well done, My good and faithful servant." Telemarketers are difficult for me, especially when they are persistent in overstepping their boundaries with my time. I quickly forget that I have ever given God any place at all in my life. We will frequently face situations in which we may have a strong resistance to civility. Always stay in a mode of allowing God to change you into His image. As I keep my mind on His presence, obedience to His ways becomes easier with each passing minute. By the end of the call with the telemarketer, all is pleasant within my soul; I am grateful that I have allowed His ways to take precedence over my sinful tendency. When you act in a Godly manner by submitting to His will, you are actually bringing Him pleasure.

And, hey, they intrude on my time—I take the opportunity to tell them about Jesus!

Day 1: Do all things without grumbling or disputing

Day 2: (15) that you may prove yourselves

Day 3: Do all things without grumbling or disputing; (15) that you may prove yourselves

Day 4: to be blameless and innocent

Day 5: Do all things without grumbling or disputing; (15) that you may prove yourselves to be blameless and innocent,

Day 6: children of God above reproach

Day 7: Do all things without grumbling or disputing; (15) that you may prove yourselves to be blameless and innocent, children of God above reproach

(verse continued)

TENA MARCHAND

THOUGHTS, PRAYERS, AND TESTIMONIES

_____

_____

_____

_____

_____

_____

_____

_____

_____

_____

_____

_____

_____

_____

_____

_____

Day 1: children of God above reproach

Day 2: in the midst of a crooked and perverse generation

Day 3: children of God above reproach in the midst of a crooked and perverse generation

Day 4: among whom you appear as lights in the world

Day 5: children of God above reproach in the midst of a crooked and perverse generation among whom you appear as lights in the world

Day 6: Philippians 2:14-15 Do all things without grumbling or disputing; (15) that you may prove yourselves to be blameless and innocent, children of God above reproach in the midst of a crooked and perverse generation, among whom you appear as lights in the world

THOUGHTS, PRAYERS, AND TESTIMONIES

Colossians 3:23–24 Whatever you do, do your work heartily, as for the Lord rather than for men; (24) knowing that from the Lord you will receive the reward of the inheritance. It is the Lord Christ Whom you serve.

It is not always easy to submit to our superiors. Perhaps we do not think alike at all, or maybe they have hurt you or have something against you. Maybe they have a very harsh or unreasonable way of dealing with you. Or maybe there are personality conflicts or clashes that make things difficult. Could it be you just don't like being under authority? Whatever the reason for the temptation at resistance, shift your focus to Whom it is that you are to serve. The more you renew your mind to this, the less difficult it is to submit to a person—because you are really serving God. He is watching to see if you are submitting to Him through those over you on earth. Anything you do to please God will not go unrewarded by Him. Keep faithful!

Day 1: Whatever you do

Day 2: do your work heartily

Day 3: Whatever you do, do your work heartily

Day 4: as for the Lord rather than for men

Day 5: Whatever you do, do your work heartily as for the Lord rather than for men

Day 6: (24) knowing that from the Lord

Day 7: Whatever you do, do your work heartily, as for the Lord rather than for men; (24) knowing that from the Lord

(verse continued)

TENA MARCHAND

THOUGHTS, PRAYERS, AND TESTIMONIES

Day 1: you will receive

Day 2: the reward of the inheritance

Day 3: you will receive the reward of the inheritance

Day 4: Whatever you do, do your work heartily as for the Lord rather than for men, (24) knowing that from the Lord you will receive the reward of the inheritance

Day 5: It is the Lord Christ Whom you serve.

Day 6: Colossians 3:23–24 Whatever you do, do your work heartily, as for the Lord rather than for men; (24) knowing that from the Lord you will receive the reward of the inheritance. It is the Lord Christ Whom you serve.

THOUGHTS, PRAYERS, AND TESTIMONIES

_____

_____

_____

_____

_____

_____

_____

_____

_____

_____

_____

_____

_____

_____

_____

_____

_____

Isaiah 55:11 So shall My Word be which goes forth from My mouth; it shall not return to Me empty, without accomplishing what I desire, and without succeeding in the matter for which I sent it.

A child told her mom that her science teacher taught that our words are molecules floating out in the universe. The mother later used this bit of information to encourage praying God's Word, if I remember correctly. She went on to tell of a man from a foreign country who heard a radio broadcast from America. In his search to find out where it originated, he discovered that the broadcast was aired twenty-five years earlier. The molecules of the words from that broadcast were still floating around out there—and was picked up by satellite to another country all those years later!

One of my sisters died a few years ago, survived by seven children and her husband. She was a very faithful and powerful prayer warrior over her family. Based on this scripture and the molecules of our words floating around out there, when I pray for her family, I end with saying, "And, Lord, I am in agreement with Linda's prayers that she prayed according to Your Word over her kids and husband." (My brother-in-law has since remarried and I faithfully pray for his precious new wife as well.) Although my sister's in Heaven, her prayers are still in action here—and they will not return to Him without accomplishing that for which it was sent. We can pray His Word over any situation. (Take caution here: Proverbs 18:21 says that "life and death are in the power of the tongue." Train yourself to always speak the positives.)

Day 1: So shall My Word be

Day 2: which goes forth from My mouth;

Day 3: So shall My Word be which goes forth from My mouth;

Day 4: it shall not return to Me empty

Day 5: without accomplishing what I desire

Day 6: it shall not return to Me empty, without accomplishing what I desire

Day 7: So shall My Word be which goes forth from My mouth; it shall not return to Me empty without accomplishing what I desire

(verse continued)

TENA MARCHAND

THOUGHTS, PRAYERS, AND TESTIMONIES

Day 1: and without succeeding in the matter

Day 2: it shall not return to Me empty, without accomplishing what I desire, and without succeeding in the matter

Day 3: So shall My Word be which goes forth from My mouth; it shall not return to Me empty, without accomplishing what I desire, and without succeeding in the matter

Day 4: for which I sent it.

Day 5: So shall My Word be which goes forth from My mouth; it shall not return to Me empty, without accomplishing what I desire, and without succeeding in the matter, for which I sent it.

THOUGHTS, PRAYERS, AND TESTIMONIES

_____

_____

_____

_____

_____

_____

_____

_____

_____

_____

_____

_____

_____

_____

_____

_____

_____

_____

_____

Matthew 22:37 (And He said to him,) "You shall love the Lord your God with all your heart, and with all your soul, and with all your mind."

I read my Bible every day, attend church regularly, encourage others, forgive readily, and faithfully give above the tithe. I routinely pray, fast, and witness of Jesus. I've seen prayers answered powerfully, and have had words of knowledge and discerning of spirits. I strive to obey His Word and repent of all sin—*so I thought*. Contrary to what it *sounds* like, I was NOT Heaven-bound. Read Matthew 7:22–23. After forty years of being a Christian, I realized that I was not serving God with my *whole heart*.

Godliness and Godly activities don't compensate for areas of *unrepentant willful sin*. Not realizing that I lost sensitivity to the Holy Spirit's conviction, I became covetous, prideful, and envious. I wasn't always completely truthful (lying). I inadvertently brought paper clips and ink pens home from work and intended to bring them back, but didn't (stealing). Would these things have cost me had I died? In Matthew 19:16–22, Jesus knew the *one thing* the rich young ruler would not give up for eternal life when he asked, "All these things I have kept; what am I still lacking?" Jesus died for all sins; we must forsake all sins. Habitual disregard of conviction will eventually distort your perception of sin as sin. Galatians 5:19–20 lists sins that those who "*practice such things*" will not go to Heaven. Felt love for God is false assurance of salvation if we're not aiming to forsake all sin with God's help.

God *is* full of mercy and grace toward us. But make no mistake—that mercy is relative to repentance, which is not only *confessing* your sins, *but also forsaking them*. I am NOT talking about repeat failures for which we have a repentant heart, and are consistently trying to overcome. It's the sins we *practice routinely*, without repentance. Two people may be guilty of the same habitual sin. One may tearfully repent with an earnest desire to change, but fail over and over again—despite attempts to stop. Extreme weakness and bondage overpower him. The Lord sees the struggle AND his *beautiful* heart. Mercy pours out on him, and he will eventually be set free by God's grace. The other person may continue to <u>*practice*</u> that same sin, but never genuinely repent (says he's sorry, but never really tries to stop). This one is *trampling on the mercy and grace of God*. There's a difference between (1) sin *overpowering and taking* the opportunity in us, and (2) *our giving* sin the opportunity as an accepted way of life (unrepentant, willful sin). Allow the Holy Spirit to show you practices and attitudes that hinder your serving God with a whole heart. He loves you so much and does not expect you to fight the battles alone. He sent the Holy Spirit to help you.

Day 1: You shall love the Lord your God with all your heart,

Day 2: and with all your soul

Day 3: and with all your soul, and with all your mind

Day 4: Matthew 22:37 (And He said to him,) "You shall love the Lord your God with all your heart, and with all your soul, and with all your mind."

THOUGHTS, PRAYERS, AND TESTIMONIES